To Team Juno

ADDICTED

To Being Broke

Let's talk about eradicating
the poverty mindset

By

Agnes Wanja

Addicted to being broke.

ISBN: 978-1-8384670-0-5

First published 2021

Dedication

I dedicate this book to everyone looking for a way out of financial hardship. There is a way, it is possible, you can do it.

First, I want to thank God for his grace and mercy on my life. I dedicate this book to my two sons, my godsons, my grand-parents (mum and dad), my family, and my close friends. It has been a long journey and those close to me know how much I have wanted to escape living in shortage, living as though there is not enough supply in the world, when, as a matter of opinion, there is an abundance of everything we need. I have always worked hard and have never hidden from my responsibilities. I have survived and learned so much from my 'broke' days that I have been inspired to write about my journey in the hope of helping those going through financial difficulties and preventing others from making the same mistakes. I want to experience the other side, to live in abundance. I have always been hungry to be better, do better, become better; I hope that my children will do better, experience better relationships and especially, that they will be financially wise.

My journey has been amazing, and the ups and the downs have enabled me to create this book. Neither my children nor I ever went without a meal or a roof over our heads, and for that I am forever grateful. I have been humbled by my life journey and the knowledge that it could have been totally different, for better or for worse, if my grandmother had not decided to raise me as her own child.

My life is blessed; before I was formed in my mother's womb God said, 'For I know the plans I have for you, plans for your well-being, not for disaster, to give you a future and a hope'. For this reason, I live my life with a spirit of power, love, and a sound mind.

Contents

Introduction

I was next in the queue at my local corner shop when I overheard the young lady in front of me first asking and then begging the shopkeeper to let her have credit on her electricity key until the next day. She begged and pleaded with the shopkeeper until he agreed. I could not judge her situation. I was next in line to top up my electricity key (which plugs into a pay-as-you-go meter) with £6. Yes, £6, which was all I could afford at the time; I had planned this to last the next two days until I was due to receive money again.

When I returned home, I questioned myself: is this normal? Is it right not to have enough money to top up your electricity key? Is it acceptable to live two days at a time, financially? Is it normal to have a full-time job and be broke each month, two days after payday?

You see, the problem is not the lack of money, but the lack of financial literacy. The lack of a basic understanding of money matters and effective money management skills; the inability to calculate how much of your money you can spend and how much you should keep aside for a rainy day.

The Money Advice Service (MAS)[1] estimates that 8.3 million adults in the UK are living with problem debt and 22 percent of UK adults have less than £100 in savings, making them highly vulnerable to a financial shock such as losing their job or incurring unexpected bills (Independent 2019). I have

[1] Free and impartial money advice, set up by government - Money Advice Service (https://www.moneyadviceservice.org.uk/en)

been one of those 8 million for most of my adult life, and I am only now edging out of that number.

I am still on a journey of understanding and managing the little amount of money I have. It has been a long, hard process, but I was unable to confront the problem until I admitted there was one. I hope this book sparks conversations about money and ensures that our future generations have a better understanding of healthy money management.

Chapter One

Cycle of Deprivation

'My car was clamped this morning (a clamp is fixed to one of the wheels so that it cannot be driven; this generally happens because of an outstanding payment of one kind or another). What upsets me the most is that I parked the car in a particular parking space so that if it did get clamped, the driver's side was away from my neighbours' view so no one would see it. Apparently, because of how the tyre was angled, the clampers had to clamp the passenger side, which was in full view of the block of flats where I live. The battle is a lot; the struggle is manageable when it's within me, but when it's out there for the whole world to see it becomes a bigger fight.

On a day like this I feel like giving up the car, giving up the fight, giving up the journey to success, just stopping and living a simpler life. I feel tired, I feel so drained mentally, emotionally, and physically, and I have a migraine.

I pleaded with the bailiffs until they took the clamp off my car and I promised them a payment at the end of the week on payday, even though I know I won't have enough money for this ticket plus the other one from last week. I need a miracle, please God, to make all my debts disappear' (notes from my phone dated 2017).

When you think of the word 'addicted', how do you feel? What comes to mind? Some might hear or read 'addicted' and look away. It is one of those words we have been taught to relate to drugs, alcohol, or sex, and in more recent times we have become addicted to our phones, social media, computer games, fast food etc. It's not a word that we think of in relation to being BROKE. What could entice anyone to be poor, let alone addicted to being broke?

The reason I chose the title of this book is because it describes my situation. I was addicted to being broke, yet I did not realise it for many years. 'Poor' was my mindset!

As a mother of two children and working full time, I survived on mental calculations of money in/money out; it seemed an efficient system, and it had worked for years, or so I thought. I subsisted on a weekly income from the government: child benefit (payable if you're responsible for bringing up a child while earning less than a certain annual sum); tax credits, (payments given to families on a low income); a contribution from the children's father; a full-time monthly wage, and my side hustle as a hairdresser.

On paper, this would appear to be a practical system, relying on multiple income streams (financial advisers always say, 'never depend on a single income.') I understood that there would never be enough money to always be able to do everything I wanted or needed to do. However, my mindset was always 'My money is going to run out', my attitude was 'There is always something to pay for' or 'Something to buy'. So, imagine someone who has all the latest gadgets, likes to buy nice stuff, the best quality, and wants to pay full price for everything... that's not me. Now imagine someone who has their priority and non- priority bills paid and up to date, enjoys regular trips to the shopping mall or often shops online for items such as clothes and shoes... no, still not me! My money was always spent on food, playing catch up with the bills, and then on the kids: yes, school dinners, school uniform, activities, swimming lessons, new shoes/trainers, birthdays, the list goes on. I have never really been one to splash out on myself ... well, not since becoming a parent!

So, to give you a clearer picture, this is what my typical week looked like. On Monday I usually start on a negative, being one day away from receiving some money - you know what that's like! A day full of anxiety hoping that I'll make it through without any surprises. On Tuesday, £35 hits my account, and my thought process starts… 'Okay I need to top up my electricity key, I need to buy food, and I need to pay the school for breakfast club'.

First, I stop at the supermarket on my way to work to get something small such as a croissant for breakfast. As I enter, I remember that I need washing up-liquid, milk, and toilet rolls. So, I start picking these things up and by the time I check out at the till I'm £20 down! 'Oh, okay that's not what I had planned when I left the house, but the day must go on', I would say to myself '…at least I still have £15 to top up the electricity and pay the school'. As the end of day approaches, I get into the car and realise that I need to get petrol, so the calculations begin again. If I get £8 petrol, I can still get £6 of electricity and have a pound left. As I drive to the petrol station, I am running through the situation in my head, feeling embarrassed to buy such a small amount of petrol; my brain is in overdrive. This is what I mean when I say, 'The battle is a lot; the struggle is manageable when it's within me, but when it's out there for the whole world to see it becomes a bigger fight'. Absent-minded and embarrassed to be putting in £8 worth of petrol, deep in thought … for how much longer will I be short of money…? I accidentally put in £9. #sigh… this was not the plan. My next stop is the corner shop to top up with my £6 and happy days! The breakfast fees will have to wait until next week. My mind will now settle on the fact that I won't receive any more money until Thursday.

In bed on Wednesday night, I calculate precisely how the money coming in tomorrow will be spent. Thursday comes, and I have £96 in my account – oh, my excitement! I've already planned what to do with this money, so within 6 hours of waking up, my account is back to £0. It's the same thing over and over again. I repeat the same thought processes without a thought-out plan. I just spend until I have no more to spend. Then, at the end of the month: £1500. Oh, this money must last a good while. First, all the direct debits are paid, the monthly payments, the rent, and then the debts: all those phone calls I receive throughout the month to which I promise payment at the end of the month because 'That's when I get paid'. By the end of payday, I am hanging on to the £220 I have left and trying to decide which is the most important of the remaining things left to pay. I can't forget about the other direct debit payments that leave my account on the first of the month. And most importantly, the surprise payments that sometimes occur during the month, such as bailiff fees. By the second of the month, I am waiting for Tuesday and Thursday and payday again.

Some people are always broke but don't work or have a business or a source of income, so you have some understanding of why they're broke all the time. I have always worked. I have always been on my feet ready to take on anything that could be exchanged for money. I took up hairdressing as a hobby: I would earn cash from it here and there, but it was not a guaranteed income. However, the truth is that even if I had one client a day, the money is always going to run out at some point. There is a lovely quote that says, 'Those who spend too fast never grow rich'. I'm not sure I could even identify exactly where the money is going. If you are reading this, thinking that it sounds familiar;

that it could be you, your friend, your sister, wife, husband, brother, or someone else you know, be sure to get them a copy of this book and encourage them to join this journey and learn with us.

I had my first son at the age of 21 and my second at the age of 24, so I pretty much had to grow up very quickly and become a responsible adult at a young age. I developed a routine of earning and spending money and my main aim was to make sure whatever money I had lasted until the next time I had some. This pattern gradually became a habit – an acquired pattern regularly followed until it has become almost involuntary[2]. It did not matter how much I had left, I felt it was okay to spend it as long as it took me to the next income day. I didn't always make it to the next income day and then I was left with no option but to borrow from the 'bank of mum' and sometimes from friends.

There were so many times, countless times, that I said to myself 'That is it! I am not going to be this broke again! I am going to save my money.' Yet I continued to find myself in the same place, broke, time and time again.

As I got older, realisation dawned that it was not okay to borrow money from family and friends, especially since I had a full-time job. I was probably earning more than the people I was borrowing from. There had to come a time for change.

---

2 Dictionary.com, *s.v.*, "habit," accessed January 11, 2020, https://www.dictionary.com/browse/habit

The lack of money and of money management skills affected all areas of my life, as a parent and as an individual. I was not able to make any plans for the future (even if the future meant the following week), but all plans were limited because they depended on whether I had any money on the day to be able to go ahead. Having no money, or a severe lack of it, meant that I was always last minute with everything because I was constantly waiting on my next income day. A typical example is when my older son needed ingredients for food technology at school. We would typically be buying them on the morning of the lesson, Thursday morning, which is when I received some money. Yes, I was that lady running up and down the supermarket aisles first thing in the morning, searching for the ingredients and rushing the kids to get ready; everything was chaotic, and that chaos was getting all too familiar.

I think the reason it took me such a long time to realise that my way of living was a problem, was because I was restricted by my limited knowledge. I was not surrounded by wealth or people who were doing extraordinary things to create lives that were better than the one I knew. It was a cycle of deprivation (the poor breeding the poor). I shared daily stories of the struggle and was so proud of how I got through the day with a minimal amount of money. There was a period of my life when I was proud of myself for getting my weekly shopping for £20 from one of the major supermarkets rather than one of the cheaper ones, and I bragged so much. I didn't realise that I was becoming accustomed to living in poverty. Don't get me wrong, bargain hunting is a good thing, but there is a difference between bargain hunting and only having pennies to spend. The struggle was real and is still real for many people: that is one of the reasons this book is so important for me. I knew I had to break out of the cycle or at least try to do things that would produce a different outcome and enable me to move forward with a better understanding into a better life.

Throughout my journey, I have been excited about having it all. Having financial freedom, a successful business, providing for my loving family, a lovely home, a nice car, you know … just living the life! When I decided I was going to change my future for the better I started to look at the research and listen to many motivational speakers. During my journey, I took a liking to motivational speakers and events. I love attending motivational events and networking. It is almost like the form of escapism you experience when going to the cinema. I attended many motivational events, and in 2012 I was invited to a 3-day event where I got to listen to some fantastic speakers; the line-up included Tony Robbins (American author, coach, motivational speaker, and philanthropist) and Donald Trump (at the time, the businessman and now, the ex-US President!). There were so many excellent speakers, I wish I could name them all. That event changed something in me. I went home with words such as 'love what you do', and 'a lot of people can't handle pressure, but a lot of people can' ringing in my ears. Listening to Tony Robbins was an experience that I will remember forever. I literally jumped up and down, thinking 'Is this what rich people do? Have fun with everything?' It was an amazing show; he played loud music at random points and asked members of the audience to get up and greet a stranger. I decided at that point that I would incorporate that element if I were ever to host events. Tony Robbins spoke about 'state' explaining that your state is everything. Before you do anything measure your state, your energy, and decide what your story is. He said one thing that has stayed with me ever since, 'We are afraid of failing, but fail anyway'. Attending motivational events became a regular occurrence for me because I enjoyed them so much. I felt at home until I started to realise that I was on the wrong side of the venue. I started to feel that I belonged on the stage, that I was called to motivate others, and that awakening was the start of my journey. It confirmed to me that my life has a greater purpose and (in case you haven't realised it yet) your life has a greater purpose too. Through my personal development journey, I found the likes of Les Brown, Brian Tracey, Lisa Nichols, and many other motivational speakers who encouraged and inspired me.

For many years I found comfort in surviving my situation. I found a way to manage with little or no money most of the time. I was always in survival mode. Only when I started reflecting on my actions did I begin to see how far I was going in the wrong direction. Sometimes you can be going so fast, always moving, and always doing things, but in the wrong direction. When I started reflecting, I began with why? Why did I take a loan for £1700 and pay back £184.25 every month for 24 months which equalled a total payment of £4,422, including interest of £2,722. This sounds like something a crazy person would do, the maths just does not add up! But yes, that's what I did (more on this story in Chapter Three). It was my constant questioning of the status quo that allowed me to look at my situation and the example I was showing to the younger generation (my kids) and consider what I could do to create generational wealth so that that cycle of deprivation would be broken.

As much as I had wished, closed my eyes, and hoped and prayed for a miracle to change my situation, it could not have changed before I had developed myself, my mindset, my circle, my vision, my dreams and most importantly, my faith, and the ability to believe that change can happen. Sometimes when you are deep in a dark situation, it can feel as though there is no point, and there is no way out. I can promise you that there is.

Reflection:

That day in the corner shop purchasing a small amount of electricity was not the first time. However, because I was hungry for change, I was able to identify the daily activities that held me back from living a better standard of life.

After reading Chapter One what are your reflections?

____

____

____

Celebrations: I celebrate the fact that I took action to start a journey of change. What could you celebrate?

____

____

____

Encouragement: I want you to understand that time is sometimes misunderstood. Just because you have been living a particular way for many years, it does not mean you cannot change for the better.

Note to self, what encouragement do you need?

____

____

____

Challenge

You have reached the end of Chapter One. I would like to invite you to take a challenge.

Choose an amount of money to put away after you have read each chapter.

£1 × 10 = £10

£5 × 10 = £50

£10 × 10 = £100

Once you have chosen your amount, I challenge you to put it aside after each chapter you complete. You will find the next step after the last chapter.

Remember this is for you and your own journey.

Chapter Two

The Consequences

'Every action has a reaction, they say. Cause and effect: the cause of my problems has been not understanding money and not being able to manage money; the effect has been a continuous cycle of deprivation, of debt and self-denied personal growth. It took me a very long time to understand what had been going on. Still, how long it took is not really important, but that I finally managed to start the journey and can offer help to someone else who is experiencing the same struggle.'

They say money does not buy happiness: I say it can provide one of the means of happiness which is paid bills. Money is not the important factor here; it's the management of money that matters. As a young adult I remember hearing that credit cards were bad, and that debt was bad, but I never heard *why* they were bad. I grew up avoiding credit cards. I did not have any financial education. I lacked understanding of how money worked. I had a subconscious attitude that money should be spent.

Sometimes when I asked for something when growing up, I remember being told to wait until the end of the month. I knew that I did not want my life to follow the same pattern, but if anything, I fell into an even more destructive cycle, because I initiated the habit of borrowing money from people and companies to make ends meet.

Such a habit forces you into the worst possible place, especially if you have dependents, such as your children. I would budget so that my money would last until I was due to receive more. The problem is that I was simply gambling. I was gambling with the chance that I would not need anything other than what I had planned for.

So why did my car get clamped? I received a parking ticket for £60, reducing to £30 if paid within 14 days. But, as we know, every single penny of my money was accounted for each week. An extra £30 was an impossible stretch for my virtually non-existent budget. So, my mindset was that I would deal with this at the end of the month when I was due to receive a larger amount of money, when it was possible to produce £60. The end of the month would come around and that £60 would be impossible to squeeze out of an already over-stretched budget. So, I would push it back to next month, and the next month would come and the same thing would happen. And then a letter from the bailiff company arrives, making me aware that they had been passed my file. At this point, panic sets in and I start to take things more seriously. I call the company and explain the situation to them. I don't like playing the victim, but in this case, I would use my 'I am a single mum' and 'low income' cards to buy some sympathy points. However, the process I had begun continues, because now I make further promises. I agree to a plan to split the debt into several payments. As we know, my budget is already stretched to breaking point, so agreeing to those payments was setting myself up for failure. Fast forward some weeks later and there we have it; the car is clamped.

What I find fascinating about this process is that I could not make provision to make a £30 payment, I could not make provision to make a £60 payment or a payment plan of £120 a month, yet I agreed to make provision to pay £450 overall (including fines) to get the car released. It reveals the utmost incompetence in understanding and managing money. This was the level I was fixed at for so many years. I know I am not alone in this because if I were, the bailiffs would not be in business. According to Creditfix, (a company that helps people solve debt problems) local governments across England and Wales passed more than 1.1 million parking fines to bailiffs for collection during 2018/19 – a 21% increase on the previous year.[3]

My problems escalated when I started taking out loans and catalogue credit. I had just moved into a new unfurnished flat, and it was not easy starting from scratch with a new baby and being so young. When we first moved in, we settled for second-hand furniture and made do with what we had. Eventually, I started replacing the old with new. When I was approved for my first catalogue, it felt like I had won a prize, there was so much excitement. Overnight I had a new bed. I had a new fridge/freezer. I had a new pair of shoes.

[3] 21% spike in number of parking fines transferred to bailiffs - Creditfix (https://www.creditfix.co.uk/blog/21-spike-in-number-of-parking-fines-transferred-to-bailiffs/)

All of a sudden, I started to feel like I could 'keep up with the Jones's'. The feeling of being able to 'buy' these things without paying was terrific. I remember thinking 'Wow! Why did no one tell me about these catalogues before? I could have had that new pair of trainers ages ago'. I applied for a loan and was approved just like that. I found that these methods of obtaining short term funding for non-essential items were the easiest ways to get into debt. They seem so useful when the deposit lands in your account, and it feels so good when you take delivery of goods that you have not yet paid for.

This way of living becomes a habit as you get used to receiving things without paying for them. In other words, you start to obtain things that you CANNOT afford. This is called living on credit. However, reality hit me when I began receiving the statements. Wide-eyed, I would scan to the bottom to find out how much I needed to pay: the first payment was fine, paid on time! The second payment was absolutely fine, paid on time! And after I had made a few monthly payments on time I was rewarded with a higher credit limit both by the credit card companies and catalogues. My days! I felt that life could not get any better at this point. I found more ways of getting credit and bought more new things.

Having one credit account that cost £33 per month did not seem too bad at the time. The problem escalated when I had six different accounts to pay, each ranging from £12 to £33 a month; that's when things began to crumble.

I began to struggle big time, giving one excuse after another to my creditors. But it felt like the demands were never-ending.

One by one, I started missing payments, the late payment fees became bigger than the original payments, and just like that, I lost control over my finances. It kept on getting worse and worse. When my car broke down and I could not afford to repair it, I had to give it up as I had bought it on credit. I was working just to pay my debts. Without realising it, I was suffering; my emotions were clearly being affected by the experience I was living through. I became more serious and less of the happy-go-lucky girl that I once was. Who can you talk to? How do you start a conversation with 'I am in so much debt' unless you're talking to someone who can help you out of the situation?

I used to joke around with friends about 'being broke', laugh and complain that it wasn't fair; the credit facilities were a trap. I had all the excuses for being in debt. My situation was very bad but because I knew there were other people in the same position, or even worse, it did not seem so bad. It almost became the norm for me. I was running behind with all my bills, including my priority bills.

I was seriously in arrears with the rent, and I was served notice to leave my property. I had to go to court not once, but twice over three years to fight to keep my home. When I received my first eviction notice, I was advised by a friend that I could apply for a 'stay of execution', which is a court order to temporarily suspend the execution of a court judgment or other court order. This would give me a chance to get my case heard at court. This was a situation that I could never have imagined finding myself in. I was a young parent whose life had spiralled out of control. I found myself in court for the first time, in front of a judge. I tried to explain my side of the story after the landlord's representative had given all the facts. I gathered myself together, but as I started trying to explain myself, I broke down in tears. I could have cried a river, but the landlord's representative was there to do a job and the judge was there to do a job and thank God! it was *this* judge who saw me through this one. I was given a chance to make a repayment that was affordable to me. I was able to keep my home, go back to it and appreciate the little I had. If the worst-case scenario had happened, my family would not have been able to accommodate us, and my babies and I would have been left out on the street. This was a terrible time in my life - rock bottom. No car, just about hanging onto my home, no more credit cards, no more catalogues, no more credit. I was not even able to get a phone on a contract, nor could I get a current account. Just like that, I went from having an excellent credit rating to an extremely poor credit rating.

At this point in my life, I did not really understand the importance of having a good credit file.

I remained in the same cycle for many years. As the kids got bigger, they started to understand that mum was always broke. That's when the truth really hit home! One evening I was watching TV with my younger son, and he said to me 'Those people on telly have money because they don't have kids, you have to spend all your money on us', and that made me feel like a failure: the kids knew that I didn't have money. They had probably heard me talk how my money was spent. That is when I knew that change had to happen, and it had to happen right then.

My boys were in primary school at this time and they loved it. Every day I would ask them how school had been, and they would tell me how it was. Sometimes they had bad days or felt that they were being picked on by the teachers. I would ask them 'Do you want me to go and speak to the teacher?' and if the answer were 'Yes', I would be at the school the next morning asking for an appointment with the teacher or the headteacher. As time went on, I started falling behind on payments for the breakfast club and the after-school club, and the boy's lunch money. I owed the school money, and I could not face going there to complain when my sons reported their unhappiness to me. I simply could not face the embarrassment. I felt ashamed of myself and as though I was living a lie. I would wake up in the morning, drop the kids to school and go to work looking like I had things under control; but the reality was far from that. I could not understand why I was trapped in a cycle of poverty.

I thought to myself, 'I'm smart, I'm positive, I listen to positive role models, I know many amazing quotes, so why am I still in this rat race?' A rat race is an endless, self-defeating, or pointless pursuit.[4]

The term is commonly associated with an exhausting, repetitive lifestyle that leaves no time for relaxation or enjoyment.' And then the penny finally dropped that I was in a situation that I mentally and physically had to get out of. I realised that positive thinking wouldn't do it, and that I had to step out, walk right out of it, two-step out, moonwalk out, however I did it, I had to make that move.

---

[4] Rat race - Wikipedia (Rate Race (2020, January 11) In *Wikipedia*)

I was on the phone to one of my friends whilst in the shop buying electricity and topping up my Oyster card. We were having a general conversation, talking about credit cards. 'Can I have six pounds on this and three pounds on this please?' I said to the shopkeeper and at the other end of the phone my 'friend' burst out laughing and said, 'Please don't tell me you are topping up your gas and electric!' I hung up the phone, firstly, because I felt disrespected: how dare someone who was supposed to be my friend laugh at me? Secondly, I was doing my best to make ends meet and didn't need someone else's mockery, and thirdly, I was not going to embarrass myself further by admitting I was indeed topping up my electricity and Oyster card.

The situation kept on hitting home, and one of the last pushes was when I was with my younger son topping up the electricity with £8, and he said, 'Why do you not just put the whole £10 on it?' At that moment I realised he had seen the pattern and that if I didn't change it, soon enough that way of living would become embedded in my boys, a habit they had picked up, and in my eyes, such a habit would be a continuation of the cycle of deprivation.

I like my job, but I don't like my job. I'm sure this sounds familiar to many of you. I like doing what I do, but I don't like having to be there Monday to Friday 9 to 5:30, waiting for pay day and then doing it all over again: it felt like something that did not fit with what I wanted my life to be. However, it did not bother me enough to make a change. I was still in and out of that office with a smile on my face, the happiest person there, cheering people up. The contradiction was that I was not happy, although I seemed happy. There was no contradiction about the fact that I didn't have any money.

What motivated me to write this story was the passion I found for financial education. I cannot tell you how many events I attended, all in the pursuit of becoming a success and most importantly, gaining financial freedom. I went from event to event, read books and watched YouTube videos. I was not able to move forward until I realised that I was operating at the wrong level. I was diving into water that was too deep for me. I was playing games that I had not attended practice for. I was trying to be a millionaire when I could not even keep hold of the small amount of money that passed through my hands each day. How do you go from 0 to a million with nothing? Well, do I wait to win the lottery? How long do I wait? Could I get a job that pays well? There are many ways to do it, but if I cannot keep £10, I cannot keep £100 or £1000, so how can I get to a million? This was when I woke up to the fact that there was so much more to the journey. I had to change my behaviour, my mindset, and my understanding.

During my journey, I came to the realisation that there is no quick way to become financially wise or master money management skills. It's not how much you earn that matters; it is how much of it you keep! If you are on a salary of £25,000 per annum and at the end of the year you do not even have £2,500 to show for it, how can you prove how much you earned without bringing out your payslip? If, on the other hand, you're earning £12,000 per annum and at the end of the year you have £1,200 put away from that salary, is that not better? This is the mindset that I had to develop.

Reflection: Not understanding money management impacted so many areas of my life and made it very difficult to focus on the other essential elements of life.

After reading Chapter Two what are your reflections?

____

____

____

____

____

____

Celebrations: I celebrate the fact that I now have a little more understanding of how to make a change in my financial journey. What do you celebrate?

____

____

____

Encouragement: It can get better and you can develop a better mindset. You can set yourself free from financial struggles just by changing some aspects of your understanding and relationship with money.

What habits do you need to change or reconsider?

____

____

____

____

Chapter Three

What about Money?

'Overcoming poverty is not a gesture of charity. It is the protection of a fundamental human right, the right to dignity and a decent life.' — Nelson Mandela, former President of South Africa.

Before I explain why I feel it's important for us to talk about the matter of poverty mindset, and then move on to the steps that I took to begin implementing changes in my journey, let's have a look at some key explanations.

According to Positive Money[5] a not-for-profit research and campaigning organisation (2011), money is an object that is generally accepted as payment for goods and services and repayment of debts in a given country or socio-economic context. The main functions of money are distinguished as a medium of exchange; a unit of account; a store of value; and, occasionally, a standard of deferred payment.

---

[5] https://positivemoney.org/about/who-we-are/

According to the Joseph Rowntree Foundation (JRF)[6]'poverty means not being able to heat your home, pay your rent, or buy the essentials for your children. It means waking up every day facing insecurity, uncertainty, and impossible decisions about money. It means facing marginalisation – and even discrimination – because of your financial circumstances. The constant stress it causes can lead to problems that deprive people of the chance to play a full part in society'.

According to Business Blogs[7], the poverty mentality is a mindset that people develop over time based on a strong belief that they will never have enough money. This mindset is driven by fear and can cause poor financial decision-making. Some common characteristics of poverty mentality include being constantly worried about money or thinking about it often, worrying about how to work for it, making decisions based on fear and thinking small rather than big.

Self-limiting beliefs are ideologies we develop about ourselves as individuals which we use to hold us back from achieving our dreams or becoming better versions of ourselves. I remember before I went back to university, I had a self-limiting belief that I could not write essays. I had always believed this, and it was not until I went to university and wrote my first essay that it was confirmed that there was no truth to that belief.

---

[6] https://www.jrf.org.uk/our-work/what-is-poverty

[7] https://www.businessblogshub.com/2012/10/do-you-have-a-poverty-mentality/

According to Investopedia[8], financial literacy is the ability to understand and effectively apply various financial skills, including personal financial management, budgeting, and investing. Financial literacy helps individuals become self-sufficient so that they can achieve financial stability.

Money is necessary because it means fewer financial worries. Money is a tool because it allows flexibility in life to do things as and when you want; money is vital because it allows for a wider variety of products and services. The more money you have, the more people you can help in different ways.

A creditor is an entity (a person or institution) that extends credit by giving another entity permission to borrow money intended to be repaid in the future. Creditors can be classified as either personal or real. People who loan money to friends or family are personal creditors.

A debtor is a person or enterprise that owes money to another party.

Good debt vs bad debt. A simple rule is if it increases your net worth or has future value, it's good debt. If it doesn't do that and you don't have the cash to pay for it, it's bad debt.

Priority debts are debts that can cause you particularly serious problems if you don't do anything about them. These can include but are not limited to rent /mortgage, council tax, gas, and electricity.

---

[8] https://www.investopedia.com/articles/investing/100615/why-financial-literacy-and-education-so-important.asp

Non-priority debts include debts that can have a significant impact on your credit file, such as credit cards, loans, and catalogue credit.

Throughout my journey and the writing of this book, it was continuously confirmed that I had many self-limiting beliefs which were not allowing me to grow and did not allow me to understand that I could be living a different kind of life. I had self-limiting beliefs because when I looked at my situation, I knew I was capable of doing better, but I almost did not believe I could do better. Self-limiting beliefs can sometime be the thin line between what you think is possible and what you know is possible. Poverty may not necessarily be due to lack of money, but the outcome of thinking in a certain way could produce a poverty mindset. I can only tell my story and say yes, I had a lack of financial education which, together with my poverty mindset led me to a life of shortage. If I look up the many definitions of poverty mindset, my situation certainly ticked a few boxes.

When you know within yourself that you have the capabilities to achieve greater than anything you have achieved so far you want firstly to provide for your family and then you want abundance in every area of your life. Still, there is something within you that tells you it's not possible, not today, not for you. You can change your limiting beliefs by allowing yourself to believe new things. Challenge your self-limiting beliefs by asking yourself why? Why do you think those things? Challenge them every day until there is no more room for them within your mind.

I wrote this book because I was tired of always running out of money, always having to make excuses about why I couldn't go out or explain why I couldn't pay for things in one payment. I then decided that there would be little point in going through that life, complaining through it, but not growing or changing through it. The vision is that we can all open our eyes and see that money is such a small element of life but yet controls so much of life, and if we can explore and increase our financial education or knowledge then let's do it! I am not an expert in financial education but what I have learned is in the table below. What I want to do as well as celebrate my journey to success is to convey to others that it's not how much money you make or have, but how you manage and maintain the amount. If you are graced to live to over 80 years of age, will the way you live now sustain you? I know it would not have worked for me, and that is why change was needed.

1	+	1	=	2
1	+	2	=	3
3	-	1	=	Savings
1	-	1	=	0
1	-	2	=	Debt
1	-	3	=	Stupid

In a simplified form, the first half of the table above illustrates my understanding of how money works. Constantly adding to what you have is proof of increase and a potentially healthy cash flow. We also have to consider expenses which are sometimes unavoidable. If you have a good balance of incoming and outgoing money (outgoing being less than incoming), then you have a healthy cash flow which makes it easier to maintain a stable financial situation.

The second half of the table shows what happens when the balance is not met. When you earn and spend the same amounts, so you are left with nothing or your spending is more than your income, so you are in constant debt, and due to the debt, you try to borrow money to keep afloat. This is where I was for a long time, but it's a joy to know there is a way out of that cycle.

Finances affect many areas of our lives. As I explained in the previous chapter, even planning for the very near future (i.e., next week) can be affected. Wait, let me put this in context. Money is one of the top three reasons relationships break down, money impacts on our wellbeing; money impacts on the opportunities we can afford. Lack of financial literacy is linked to poverty and most importantly, a poverty mindset. According to Full Fact, which is an organisation that fights for the right information to reach the people who need it most (Sep 2019), an estimated 14.3 million people are in poverty in the UK. 8.3 million are working-age adults, 4.6 million are children, and 1.3 million are of pension age. Around 22% of people are in poverty, and 34% of children[9]. These numbers astonished me because, during my time in deep debt, I felt so ashamed, as though I was the only one facing this sort of financial hardship. Truth be told, it could be your best friend

---

[9] Poverty in the UK: a guide to the facts and figures - Full Fact (https://fullfact.org/economy/poverty-uk-guide-facts-and-figures/)

suffering, it could be one of your family members, it could be your neighbour, these 14.3 million people are all around us, and unless we make this subject more accessible and not a conversational taboo, we will not be able to help each other.

There are many reasons why people fall into debt, mine was a lack of financial education. For others it may be due to life changes including relationship breakup, living beyond available means, lack of emergency funds, avoiding reminder letters, mental health issues, the list is endless, and the results are not to be ignored.

What I want to explore here is not how much money you are making, but the fact that no matter how little or how much you earn, a poverty mindset can have the same impact. If you earn £1000 or receive £1000 in benefits each month, is it acceptable for you to spend the whole £1000 each month? If you earn £3500 each month and you spend £3500 (or more sometimes, using your credit facilities) is that ok? Are you wealthy, or are you broke? Do you have an abundance mindset or a poverty mindset? You see, questions are good because they seek a new level of understanding. 'Proper preparation is the key to our success. Our acts can be no wiser than our thoughts. Our thinking can be no wiser than our understanding.' — George S. Clason author of The Richest Man in Babylon.

It is those sorts of questions that led me to write this book. It's because I challenged my limiting beliefs that I was able to challenge myself to get rid of them. I decided that if I could make those changes for myself it was possible that I could help others challenge their self-limiting beliefs and help to make change happen for the people around me, the people in my community and others further afield.

Health wealth

Different communities understand and talk about mental health in different ways. In some communities, mental health problems are rarely spoken about and can be seen in a negative light. This can discourage people within the community from talking about their mental health and perhaps be a barrier to engagement with health services. Why are we talking about mental health? Because the effect of a lack of understanding about money matters, the stresses from mismanaging money and sometimes not having enough money to get through the day affects our mental health. According to the charity, Money and Mental Health, almost one in five (18%) people with mental health problems are also in problem debt.[10]

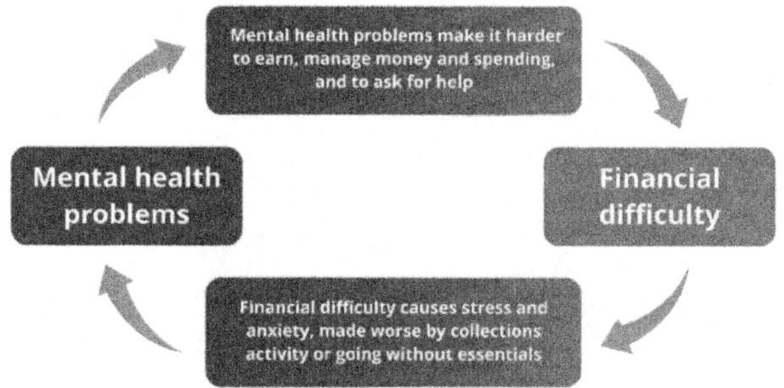

When I was deep in debt I still had to go to work, I still had to look after my children, and I still had to show up at university,

[10] https://www.moneyandmentalhealth.org/money-and-mental-health-facts/#

I still had to chase my dream. Still, my mind was constantly whirring with 'Are the bailiffs coming tomorrow?', 'Do I need to pay the rent tomorrow? I need the rent money to pay for another debt', 'I need to pay for the kids' after school club so that I can continue to go to work', 'I need to put petrol in my car otherwise I can't make it to work tomorrow'. That is not a healthy mindset. That kind of mindset reduces the ability to concentrate on just one thing or the most important thing. That kind of mindset encourages constant excessive fears and worries. That kind of mindset needed to be changed. When you get used to a particular way of living or going too far in the wrong direction, it is that little bit harder to stop and start thinking in new ways or to start going in the right direction.

Unfortunately, talking about how broke you are is not a common subject and when discussed is often brushed over with 'Yeah I'm so broke this month'.... But no one discusses their lack of financial education or understanding of how to keep on top of their finances. No one talks about how they are constantly broke, that they have no food because they are trying to keep up with their car payments, that they are struggling to keep a roof over their family's heads, and these are conversations we need to have. We need to make these problems as easy to talk about as it is for someone who is trying to lose weight to get a personal trainer or join a gym. The lack of conversation and discussion needs addressing, and I hope that this book encourages us to be more open and helps to remove the stigma attached to the poverty mindset. I hope that it encourages an interest in money management and helps bring about an understanding that money worries are an issue that people can work on together or seek help for. We can get better financially. Once we understand the processes better, it does become more manageable. Once we can manage the little we have, we can work on attaining more, making our money grow and changing the outcome and habits for future generations; this is an opportunity to break the cycle of deprivation. We should bring up our children in ways they will not depart from once they grow up.

For years, I had to deal with an inability to get involved in any conversation that turned into a discussion about savings or financial stability. I comfortably said that I would be a millionaire one day, but what I had to overcome first were the obstacles to becoming a hundredaire and a thousandaire!

If you spend money before you receive it, or are always worried about money, you are operating from a poverty mindset. Your aim should be to get on top of your finances so that when you receive money, it's not all going to disappear immediately, leaving you to wait for another day.

A friend of mine once said 'Why get paid once a month when you can get paid every day?' That, to me is a wealth-building mindset. To have passive income or multiple streams of income, and not be solely dependent on one income, gives you the ability to worry less about having enough and more about how to keep your cash flow.

So now we know more about a poverty mindset, let's look at some of the reasons that people go broke and stay broke (in no particular order):

- Spending more than you earn or make / spending habits
- Earning less than you need
- One source of income

- No budget
- Depending on credit
- Trying to impress others
- Investing in the wrong things

Spending more than you make

'It's not how much you make, but how much you keep', I've heard this many times. Spending more than I had was my everyday way of living. If you look at my 2017 budget, I was over £600 in deficit each month. Come on Agnes! I say to myself now, that was ridiculous. Thank God, I survived that. In fact, because I survived month after month on this deficit, I gained confidence, and even though it often felt like a walk of shame, I still walked the walk each month. By 2018 I was able to reduce this deficit sum to just over £300. I was spending more than I was making and unless I could reverse this and start cutting out some expenses or rapidly increase my income, I would not be able to change my outcome.

Budget summary

Total income	£1,788.81
Total expense	£2,438.82
Totaldeficit	£650.01

Spending breakdown

Household bills	£1,003.33	41%
Living costs	£475.18	20%
Finance & Insurance	£587.45	24%
Family & Friends	£312.86	13%
Travel	£60.00	3%
Leisure	£0.00	0%

2017

Budget summary

Total income	£1,804.65
Total expense	£2,150.85
Totaldeficit	£346.19

Spending breakdown

Household bills	£1,268.33	59%
Living costs	£293.93	14%
Finance & Insurance	£184.00	9%
Family & Friends	£230.00	11%
Travel	£134.58	6%
Leisure	£40.00	2%

2018

Budget summary

Total income	£2,181.03
Total expense	£1,928.80
Totalsurplus	£252.23

Spending breakdown

Household bills	£1,264.00	66%
Living costs	£362.38	19%
Finance & Insurance	£92.00	5%
Family & Friends	£70.00	4%
Travel	£30.42	2%
Leisure	£110.00	6%

2019

Earning less than you need

This is one thing that took me a very long time to understand. It sounds so easy. I remember at the interview for one of my first full time paid jobs I was told what the salary would be, and I said 'Ok!' and just agreed to it. Their immediate question was 'Will that be ok?' At that time, I did not really understand the question: I had not worked out how much money I needed to live on as I was still living at home. I did not understand, and nobody told me, that when you apply for a job you need to calculate how much you will be earning minus all your expenses so that you know if it will carry you through each month. The problem with this calculation is that now I am in a position where I earn more than my expenses, it is still not enough. It is not in line with what I believe my worth to be. An employer does not necessarily pay you according to your worth but 'You get paid in direct proportion to the difficulty of the problems you solve' - Elon Musk, entrepreneur, and businessman.

One source of income

From my point of view, relying on just one source of income is the greatest gamble one can live by. If you have only one source of income and suffer job loss or become too unwell to work, you are potentially left with no income and may become dependent on state benefits or an insurance pay out if you have one in place, which then becomes your only source of income. Our ability to make money does not stay the same throughout our lives and you can't work as fast or do as much heavy lifting in your 80s as you can in your 20s. Unfortunately, due to my mindset and my basic lack of financial understanding, I constantly found myself trading my time for money, and not making enough money, therefore, trading more time working another job to make ends meet. If you trade your time for money there is a limit to how much you can earn in one day; you are paid by the hour, and there are never more than 24hrs in a day (and legally, you should not work the whole day). So, if you choose to work 12 hrs a day and you are paid £10 per hour, the maximum you will earn is £120. After tax, that is approximately £96.00 for the day, so I came to realise that the trading of time for money is not the best trade. On the other hand, if you have an item that you can sell for £10, there is no limit to how many you can sell in one day.

As mentioned in Chapter One, I had many streams of income, but I did not use this to my benefit, I just saw them as another way to add to my spending. If you do not deal with your mindset, the actions will not change. 'Whatever you hold in your mind on a consistent basis is exactly what you will experience in your life.' - Tony Robbins, author, coach, motivational speaker, and philanthropist.

No budget

For years I had no plan for how to spend my money, but I knew every last penny was already spent even before the money got to me. I had no plan to set aside money for a rainy day, I just hoped and prayed the rainy days never came. There was no focus; there was no control; there was no accountability. This is one of the reasons for financial overspending and unless you are overflowing with income or passive income, overspending will lead to debt and always being broke. Because I did not have a budget, the money came in and went straight back out with no identifiable purpose. If you take nothing else away from this book, please work out a budget. Having a budget does not mean you are broke; it means you care enough about your money to make it work positively for you and your situation.

Depending on credit

We live in a society where credit forms part of our everyday lives. As such, there is a system that keeps and records all credit you apply for. This information is then recorded on a file called your 'credit file' or 'credit history'. When I began to make credit applications, I had no idea about the 'credit file', I was of the opinion that companies just decided yes or no (bear in mind, I was only 21!). I had never owned a credit card because 'they are bad for you'. Because I lacked financial literacy, I abused my credit facility and in turn, doomed my credit future for years to follow. Campaign, a leading business media brand serving the marketing, advertising, and media communities, in their study 'The Future of Money'[11] explored the UK's attitude to finance and found that 29% of Brits have 'little or no financial knowledge' (rising to 44% among 16- to 24-year-olds), while 82% with credit card debt also have unsecured debt elsewhere.' Campaign also predicts that cash will disappear by around 2030. There is no better time than now to start understanding money, credit, and financial matters on a factual level.

Trying to impress others

One of the first cars I bought on finance was a Mercedes A-class. I part-exchanged my old car, put down a deposit and took out finance for the balance. I was made redundant at work during the term of the finance agreement, but luckily, I had taken out gap insurance which covered my payments for about six months. When I returned to work, the car broke down, and it cost more to repair than the value

[11] Brits lack financial savvy and obsessed with instant gratification (campaignlive.co.uk) (https://www.campaignlive.co.uk/article/brits-lack-financial-savvy-obsessed-instant-gratification/1590980)

of the vehicle. But I did not need that car. I could have saved up to buy one, the way I had with my first car but, I 'wanted' something that looked 'better'. However, this is not always the case. The element of affordability is the key understanding, and financial education will allow you to understand that it is okay to buy a car on finance, but it is important to get a good deal on the borrowed money so that you are not paying too much interest.

Investing in the wrong things

Investing in yourself will be one of your best and most important investments. Investing in your self-development, in your continuous education (not necessarily formal education) attending events, listening to audio, and watching videos on topics that interest you. Around one in four UK adults has no savings, according to the Financial Conduct Authority (FCA). I had such a negative mindset towards saving, even as a parent. My mindset was 'What's the point of saving, we are not guaranteed tomorrow so why keep money for it?' This has been one of the most difficult parts of my journey to financial understanding. I was unable to understand that my future is worth investing in. If you are blessed to live to over 80 years of age, wouldn't you like to be secure in the knowledge that you invested properly to secure your future? I hope I am still able to do the things I love at the age of 80, but I do not want to be in a situation where I am worried about how much money I have to get me through each month.

Reflection: Little progress is better than no progress. I am grateful that I started my budget back in 2017, as this has allowed me the opportunity to reflect on my journey.

After reading Chapter Three, what are your reflections?

____

____

____

Celebrations: I celebrate the fact that I now have money left over after all my payments have been made and this has allowed me some form of flexibility with my spending. What do you celebrate?

____

____

____

Encouragement: If you don't already have a budget form, use the one on the next page to start keeping a record of your income and expenses. You can also access one online.

Where can you start to cut back to have some money left over?

____

____

____

BUDGET FORM

Total income	
Total expense	
Total	

Items	Amount £	How often	Each month average £
Pay yourself first (your future) even if it's £10			
Rent/Mortgage			
Service charge			
Building/content insurance			
Council tax			
Gas/electric/water			
Phones/internet			
Loans/HPI/PCP			
Petrol/travel costs			
Groceries/ household items			
Clothing/footwear			
Childcare costs/ maintenance payments/ school meals			
Leisure and entertainment			
Others			
TOTAL	£	£	£

The loan that made no sense!

There are different levels of financial education. This book is designed as an entry-level introduction that could save you from potentially bad financial decisions. As I share my own experiences, I hope they can open your eyes to your own situation as well as allow you to avoid the mistakes that I have made.

Due to my lack of financial education coupled with a desperate need for money, I took out a loan for £1,700. I took this loan out from a high-interest loan company because my credit rating was very poor. I had to pay back £184.25 every month for 24 months which equalled £4,422 with interest of £2,722. During the process of taking out this loan, I did not even care how much I was going to have to pay back. The most unbelievable thing was that I could, in no way, afford this loan. When my credit file was printed, it did not show my car finance payments, but when I printed my bank statement, they were visible. Luckily, (as I thought at the time because of my desperation) I was still granted the loan. The first two repayments were fine, but as time went on it became impossible to keep up with the payments as well as my priority bills and I fell behind with them. In the end, I managed to make the 24 payments, although not within the 24 months as per the contract. After making the 24th, and to my mind the final payment, the company contacted me to advise that I still owed a further 14 payments of added interest because of the extended length of the payment plan. So, to clarify, they said I owed an additional £2,733 more than the initial loan. At this point, I made it very clear that I would not make any additional payments because they had not been specified when I initially contacted them about extending the repayments. I wrote to the company and requested that any further correspondence be made in writing and made it clear that I did not want any more phone calls from them. I know one could argue that it was in the contract I signed, but I would say that as a responsible lender you should ensure that this is further confirmed during the term of the contract and especially when communication is made to inform you that payments will not be made. The loan company totally ignored my letter. I then raised an official complaint to them, explaining that I had not received a response to my initial complaint and that I did not want to be contacted by phone. They responded to the second letter but made no reference to my initial 3-page complaint. They basically didn't care about what I had to say and insisted that I still needed to pay the rest of the money owed. It is incredible what capabilities and abilities you can develop when you choose to take things seriously. At this time, I was already on the journey of improving my financial situation, and within the letter they sent me, were details for the Financial Ombudsman (FO). I was advised that I could contact the FO for free if I were not happy with their response. This was the first time I had ever followed that kind of thought. The old me would have just decided not to pay them back and hope that it would eventually go away. I wrote to the FO, explaining the whole situation from the beginning and included all the loan company correspondence and my initial 3-page complaint letter.

My request to the company was to acknowledge that although I had struggled, I had made the 24 payments that I was contracted to pay and therefore that any further request for money should be cancelled. The FO upheld my complaint, and not only did they cancel any further payments requested from the loan company, but they also requested that the loan company refund all the interest I had paid on the loan plus 8% interest on top. Following the Ombudsman's investigation, it was found that the affordability assessment was not properly carried out and that giving me the loan had put me in a worse financial situation than I was already in.

Chapter Four

Letting go of the Old Ways and Learning New Ways

'I learned that courage was not the absence of fear, but the triumph over it. The brave man is not he who does not feel afraid, but he who conquers that fear.' — Nelson Mandela.

Fear said to me; you can't write a book, what do you know about writing a book? You are still struggling financially, and people are going to know you were broke. Faith replied by telling me to write, keep writing, word after word, no matter what you see in front of you or what you hear around you, write. The sound of faith made me feel better, and I choose to constantly feed that faith during my journey. Change is not easy and having the courage to make your vision reality is not always a straightforward journey. Change is always happening - today will be different to tomorrow. When I decided that I wanted a change, that I wanted to gain a better understanding of money I had to start working on my mindset. Come with me as I track back my steps and see how I developed my knowledge of money, especially as an adult.

When I decided to make the transition to financial education seriously, I knew I had to let my family into the truth about my situation. So, one evening after a school gathering, we met for a chat. Bear in mind that the kids were around, and I didn't want them hearing that mama was as broke as a joke.

After we had tea, biscuits, and some excellent quality cakes (I love cake!) I directed a question to my Aunty 'How do you stay on top of your finances?' She almost didn't know how to answer because it was not something she thought about. Where I had developed the habit of being left with no money, she had developed a habit of always having money, to the point that it did not play a big role in her daily life. I would think of money before I even opened my eyes, but she would open her eyes and think about breakfast, work, and dinner because lack of money did not hinder her thought or plans.

She started telling me how she dealt with her salary each month, and I can tell you, it was not what I was doing with my salary.

She has the same bill payment leaving her bank each month at the same time, and if there are any extra payments, she would know about them in advance and arrange for them to be paid accordingly. But what shocked me the most was the fact that she could save each month! A chunk of her money goes into her savings! At this point the rest of us were in total shock.

I explained to them that I think I have a problem! I am addicted to being broke! But they burst out laughing. I explained to them that if there is money in my account, I can't stop thinking about what I could do with it until it is all gone, but they just did not seem to understand what I meant. I told them that I don't have any money now and I had to 'borrow' money just to make today happen. I have already spent the £35 that will be in my account on Tuesday and today is Sunday.

They go on to ask me if I have any credit cards, I say yes, I have one. They ask what the limit is, and I say £250 and they burst out laughing, literally, with tears in their eyes saying that they didn't realise credit cards offered such low limits. I was even laughing at this point as I thought to myself, this is actually a joke. They went on to ask how I managed the credit and I told them that it had been maxed out in the first two weeks and that I am still paying it back. Oh! .... the tears were flowing again with laughter.

I started to see a clear picture of my financial status as a joke, an inferno of a joke.

My Aunty, once she had gathered herself, gave me some advice. She said I should withdraw what I need for the week and leave my card at home. As she was explaining it, I felt that I could do it, that I could get on top of my finances. I could make this happen - if she can do it, so can I.

It's said that Rome was not built in a day, so changes take time, but believe that the most important thing is to want the change.

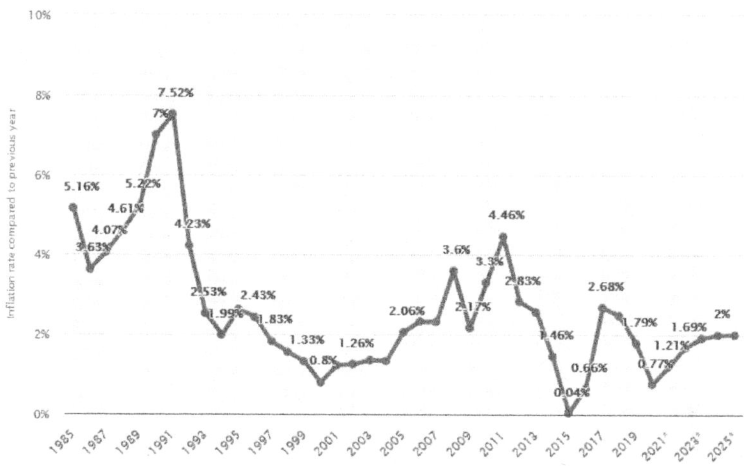

United Kingdom: Inflation rate from 1985 to 2025 (compared to the previous year)[12]

Before writing this book, I didn't pay attention to a lot of things that contribute to or dictate how money works. To be honest, I did not even care. Because of my poverty mindset, I just expected to carry on and survive on what I had. Inflation is something that every person dealing with, or in charge of household finances should be aware of. If you continue to earn the same amount of money year after year and the cost of living keeps rising year after year, you could find yourself in a place of financial struggle. This is because the value of money (i.e., you could buy more with it several years ago than you can now) has decreased, but your income has not increased. A wealth building mindset

[12] United Kingdom - Inflation rate 2025 | Statista (https://www.statista.com/statistics/270384/inflation-rate-in-the-united-kingdom/)

allows you to look deeper into these situations and be better informed to plan for your financial future. The general increase in prices and fall in the purchasing value of money should be at the forefront of your budgeting. The ability to include this factor allows you the leverage to always be in control of your finances.

The greatest thing about change is that the decision to change can happen in a moment or overnight; however, the process of change is ongoing, and it can be a long time before you see the fruits of your labour. It is a commitment to a way of living. I believe it is because I took steps to start changing my interaction with money, firstly through my mindset, and then through action, that this ongoing process of change will allow me a better financial future. It is never too late or too early to decide that financial struggle is not your portion in life. It is never too late to decide you will not be broke again. It is never too late to reach your aim and work towards a better financial future. The poverty mindset is so deeply embedded within some of us that even the idea of being able to think differently is a challenging one. It *is* a process, and one that should be understood as not being about getting rich or finding ways to be a millionaire (which are all good), but about finding a way to manage what you have now to the best of your ability. The ability to keep a record of what is working for you financially and what is not working for you; reflecting back on your budget year after year and noting the progress; being able to look at your budget and say, 'The amount of money I spend on take-aways or clothing items each month is not helping me fix my financial future'.

The understanding of short-term loss and long-term gain is key. Being able to understand that you may not be able to spend money on new shoes or a weekend break for the next six months allows you to control your chance of a better financial position in the long term. When I went back to university to do my Master's in Urban and Regional Planning which was funded by my employer, I took the decision to reduce my working hours. This put a lot of pressure on my finances and it was a difficult time, but it was my mindset during this time that kept me going. I constantly reassured myself; this is a short-term loss for a long-term gain. Once I have graduated, I will be able to pick my hours back up at work and get a pay rise: this is a long-term gain because it will give me more earning opportunities in the future.

My life journey started over three decades ago in a village called Murang'a in Kenya, where I was born. My mother passed away when I was barely months old. I was brought up by my grandparents, (who became mum and dad to me). My late grandfather was a great businessman and, from what I can remember, a very ambitious man. My grandmother is the most amazing woman I know, very charismatic, full of wisdom: she is amazing. I had a fantastic childhood full of love, and we had everything we needed.

I moved to the UK with my family just before I was a teenager, leaving my grandparents behind. As I got older, I was convinced that God had a great purpose for my life. I could not see it, I could not understand it, but I just knew that my life was meant for a great purpose. There is no way God had brought me from a small village in Kenya to live in the United

Kingdom, in London, one of the major cities of the world, to have a 9am to 5pm Monday to Friday, month on month job, without any form of financial freedom. Of course, there is nothing wrong with working this pattern, but it just did not feel right for me.

I believe we are all here to contribute to a change in the world.

So many great men and women have come into this world, changed it for the better and now have left.

We have now come into the world and are enjoying a way of living that others paved the way for; what are we doing to continue to pave the way for ourselves, our families, our children, and our children's children? What will they say when we are gone? I've been to enough funerals to know I want to have made a change before I move on to meet my creator.

I would like to believe that this book is the beginning of my contribution to the world.

I want us to celebrate the journey - after all - that's where all the fun is, that's where the trials and tribulations are, that's where you find out your true purpose in life, and that's where you find your passion, where you break a leg, a nail, your wig drops off.

Once you get to the top, you can enjoy the views, knowing that you celebrated your journey up. You did not complain all the way, you did not give up, and you did not bring others down; you carried on even though it was hard, even though it was difficult, even though no one may have believed in your vision.

The problem is not that we are not capable of achieving the best within ourselves, but that we set ourselves such small goals that when we reach them, there is no celebration and no excitement. Fear is powerful, yet powerless if you give it nothing. We feed our fears with overthinking. When I decided to change my mindset to start having more respect for money because I had begun to understand the power of it, it still took me a while to put my new mindset into action.

I didn't know this at the time, but the fear of success is actually a real thing, and overthought, can be a hurdle to success. Because I had succeeded in other things in my life, my mindset towards succeeding financially, was 'It's possible and I will do it when I am ready'. The problem is that we are never ready. If we wait until we are ready to do the things we need to do, we might never get anything done. I also felt that my financial struggle was the biggest driver of my motivation; the thing that kept me going from one job to another and from one business to another. The rat race, the lack of money somehow gave me my determination to keep going and trying new things, so I created a fear factor element in my mind that said if I succeed at managing my money and I have money and become content, what will I chase? These subconscious fears did not allow me to grow in my understanding of my finances. Fear comes in so many different forms.

First, I had to discover why - why do I want this change in my life? My why for years was based on changing my ways to 'have' money. I want to save money so that I know I have money in my account. Or I want to save money so that I can buy something. These reasons were never enough to pull me towards achieving the goal. The why was not strong enough. I was never able to keep to it or achieve it.

I decided to change my why by making my why stronger; I made my why closer to my heart.

Overthinking leaves us confused; action lets us know where we stand – the author.

Reflection: Change is a matter of thought but is not complete if not backed up with action.

After reading Chapter Four, what are your reflections?

Celebrations: This book will be here for generations to come!

What do you celebrate?

Encouragement: I want to encourage you to understand that yes, you can allow yourself to think bigger and better and, yes, you can allow yourself to not worry about money constantly.

What action do you need to take?

Chapter Five

Change in Action

You will need to have a budget, and to create one, you need to have a clear understanding of your incomings and outgoings. When I first started my journey to overcome the way of living that I had been accustomed to for most of my adult life, I started to do some research. Nearly every book, video, and podcast I read, watched, or listened to emphasised the need for a budget. But, because I already knew that I was making less than my outgoings, it was a daunting process. I was not motivated to do it, but if you want to see change, you have to keep clear records of your incomings and outgoings. Just think about it as a journey you are about to embark on - you need a map! You need to know where you are now, where you need to get to and how you will get there.

My budget allows me to identify where my money is coming from and going to. It has also allowed me to see what I can stop paying for or reduce spending on to retain more of my money. A budget allows you to see whether or not you are making progress over the years.

Using a budget as a map allows you to understand very quickly, when faced with a new cost, whether or not you can afford to engage with it. If your budget clearly indicates that you have £200 left at the end of each month, you already know that you can't afford new car finance at £250 a month. A budget allows you to control your spending and therefore equips you to stay on top of your finances.

If you feel your current source of income is not sufficient, look at ways of increasing your incomings. There are many ways this can be done, and the first is to discover whether there is the possibility of a pay rise in your current employment or if there are other higher-salaried roles that you could apply for. If you are already trading your time for money, I advise that you consider looking for an additional source of income which does not require you to trade your time directly for the exchange of money. There are a number of income streams you can develop to increase your income potential. I will discuss three.

Earned income is the money you receive in exchange for time spend at your job. I have read that JOB stands for Just Over Broke. This might be the only way you have been able to make money or the only way you are aware of. I believe the Just Over Broke statement refers to the pattern that develops when we depend on a salary. It is spent soon after we receive it, and then we go back to work and wait to get paid again. Even if you are one of the lucky few who has a great deal of money left after payment of your monthly or weekly salary, it is not a method designed to make you rich or allow you to achieve financial freedom in later life. I have been employed for the majority of my adult life. It is all well and good to collect your salary at the end of each month, but it is also important to keep an eye on your pension contributions if you are enrolled in a pension scheme with your employer. Once you reach the stage where you have more money left over at the end of each month, it may be worth considering increasing your pension contributions for your future. For some, this is as simple as getting in touch with your Human Resource department and having a conversation about the possibilities. I would also seek professional financial advice for more information regarding pension schemes.

The second potential income stream is profit income. This is income made from buying goods and selling them for more than you paid for them. You can do this alongside your job, and you don't need to start with a huge investment. I have bought small items, investing £30 at a time, and sold them on for a profit. If you find a good product, you could be in for a good profit run. You can also sell your services; although this might be a little more time consuming and might require more interaction with people. Please make sure that you understand the tax requirements if you build up a profitable business liable for paying tax.

The third potential income stream is passive income. Passive income is a form of income that does not necessarily require your presence or everyday input to generate money. An example of this is investment in a property that you rent out, affiliate marketing, dividend paying stocks or even the sale of this book! As the book is available on Amazon, I don't have to be present for sales to go ahead. This is the ultimate goal, what the speakers at the events I attended were trying to teach. This is ultimately where I want to be, to have more than once source of income and not constantly trading time for money, this is what we should all be aiming for. I'm not advising that you should give up your day job, but this could be the best way to top up your income. Now that I know what I want, I can plan how to get there.

For this section, I want you to close your eyes and think about what kind of life you would choose to live if money were no object. Then open your eyes and write down your most important vision; remember, this copy of the book is yours and no one has to see it, so you can let your self-limiting beliefs go and feel free.

Now I want you to ask yourself, what do you have to do to make this happen. What is the first step you need to take to start creating change and make things a little better than they are now?

After you have completed that first step, I want you to do the same with the next step and keep taking those steps until you reach your ultimate vision. If it wasn't possible, it would not have been your vision.

Reflection: Not every business I have started has worked out for me. I am grateful that I never gave up.

After reading Chapter Five what are your reflections?

____

____

____

____

____

Celebrations: knowing that I have started building my savings fund.
What can you celebrate?

____

____

____

Encouragement: Owning and running a business is not for everyone. Find a way of increasing your income without having to increase your exchange of time for money.

What skills do you have that can be a source of additional income for you?

____

____

____

Chapter Six

The Solution

What to do when you find yourself boxed in with all your debt? You are in your house or at work, and all you can think of are the outgoings you are not able to keep up with. Please, please, please call out, speak out, seek the help you need, whether it be financial or verbal support.

When the creditors are calling you, answer the phone. Don't ignore the calls; this is my advice and I know what it is like when you can't pay your rent in full because your salary cleared on a Friday and the rent direct debit does not come out until Monday. You just want to have a good weekend, you worked for that money, so you feel that you deserve to spend some of it. It is now Wednesday, and your landlord's number appears on your phone, and your heart drops. You are at work, your whole mood changes, and you feel the sweat dripping from your head. I know what it is like, but I ask you to pick up the phone and speak to your landlord. Tell them you are aware that your payment did not go through and ask for some extra time to make the payment. Answer the phone when your credit card company calls and speak to them, tell them if you are struggling so that they can offer you an affordable payment that may also stop the interest from increasing which will give you peace of mind. If you never face your problems, they become bigger.

Do not hide from your debts; do not try to ignore them because they won't go away. They won't dissolve, at least not for six years if they make it onto your credit file. Face them and give yourself peace of mind, knowing that you won't have a surprise visits from the bailiff at 6 am. I am telling you this because I now know that I could have avoided a lot of problems myself if I had just called the companies back. They'll call and send letters and when they cannot get an answer they will eventually knock on your door. So, do yourself a favour, speak to them and try to resolve the problem as soon as possible.

Before anything else get your priority bills in order. In my opinion, your rent or mortgage is the most important priority bill. Without a roof over your head, council tax and credit card payments do not mean much. When I had to attend court for the second time, I actually went on my lunch break. My work colleagues had no idea. I represented myself at court both times, and as my family read this, they will be in shock as they were none the wiser! The second time was the final time I would attend court for rent arrears. It was also a blessing as the housing team did not turn up, so it was just me and the judge. The judge heard my side of the story, and she praised my efforts to work and study, and allowed me to choose a suitable amount to pay on top of my weekly payment.

Don't become too reliant on housing benefit, which is given to those on low incomes to help them breach the gap between their income and their rent. These payments, as well as discretionary housing payments, are received at the 'discretion of your local authority to help towards your rent. These payments are subject to change and can stop at any point'.[13]

If you can, try to get yourself to a place where you don't need to claim for benefits. Independence from benefits allows you to budget better and take control of your housing situation. I know this is not as easy as it sounds, and I know rent can be very expensive depending in the area you live in. It does not have to happen overnight, but you can make small steps to attain this as an end goal.

Citizens Advice estimate 2.2 million households in 2019 are behind on their council tax, which is the most common debt problem they are asked to assist with. After rent or mortgage, the second priority debt is council tax, and, as stated above, it is important to communicate with your local authority if you are struggling to make payments. It can be as simple as sending them an email.

I still have arrears on my council tax account, and as it is still with the local authority, there is no interest added to the outstanding amount. The problem escalates when you choose to ignore it.

---

[13] https://assets.publishing.service.gov.uk/government/uploads/system/uploads/attachment_data/file/827510/discretionary-housing-payments-guide.pdf

You can write to your local authority to negotiate a payment plan before it gets to enforcement, and you will have a better chance of resolving it. Once the debt is passed to a debt collection agency interest will be added, and a payment plan arrangement with a debt collection agency will be more costly than an arrangement with the local authority.

When you start to learn about managing your money and understand how to start getting ahead, it is important to note that some non-priority bills and debts may be more costly. For example, if you have a credit card that isn't interest-free, you will be paying interest on the outstanding amount. It is important to get on top of those kinds of debts so that you get to keep more of your money, sooner.

I ruined my credit file at a young age, so I did not really have an opportunity to accumulate too much credit card or store card debt, which was a blessing. When I started on the journey to break my addiction to constantly being broke, I was utterly single minded, all I thought about was paying off what I needed to. I did not pay much attention to my credit file because 'I was not going to apply for credit' again! It was the least I could say in the midst of a traumatic journey and, understandably, I did not want to end up in the same place again.

First things first, I obtained a copy of my credit report on a 14-day free trial credit report site. Once you have this, save it, or print it and check it line by line, to understand each account and recorded item. Make sure you are registered on the electoral roll and that all your personal details are noted correctly. Your title, name, date of birth should all be correct.

I checked each item on my list. One by one, I contacted the companies with whom I had an outstanding balance to find out how I could resolve the payments to reduce their negative impact. You will be surprised at the results you can get simply by writing to companies and explaining your situation and why you got into arrears. Always be truthful. If you were going through a difficult time, maybe a relationship breakup, the loss of a job or other major life change, let them know. I contacted one of the banks who had reported a default on my credit file. I explained exactly what I was going through and asked if they could remove the default on my account as it was for a small amount. They wrote back and informed me that the debt was mainly made up of charges, and that they would be clearing the default on my credit report, clearing the balance, and compensating me for the inconvenience. The power of communication is unmeasurable. As my credit file started to improve, I was faced with tempting opportunities to apply for more credit cards, and my friend at work said 'Aggy, just say no, it's so easy to get the credit but so difficult to pay it back'. Unfortunately, as a creature of habit, I went ahead and took the new credit card and just as I had been warned, I fell back into the same cycle of missed payments. I then promised myself that I would not apply for more credit until I had a firm understanding of how to manage money, and particularly, that I was able to work with what I had.

What I have come to understand is that credit is important, and whether you choose to use it or not, it is better to have the option available.

The light at the end of the tunnel becomes visible once you start getting on top of your debt and paying things off; you will start to see a little bit left over at the end of the month. Please don't feel the need to increase your outgoings when this happens. This is your opportunity to start saving and keeping some of that money for yourself. Paying yourself first should be something you take pride in. After a number of trials, I am starting to get the hang of it, and it is beginning to feel normal. There is a feeling of security and ease when you know that some of the money you are working for can be kept for your future. Otherwise, you become a slave to your lifestyle. You go to work to pay your bills and don't enjoy any of what life has to offer. Make it your goal not to be a slave to your lifestyle but to benefit from your trade of time for money.

Reflection: Looking at my credit report and keeping an eye on my credit score became a form of social media for me.

After reading Chapter Six what are your reflections?

____

____

____

____

____

Celebrations: I celebrate my openness to learning new things. What do you celebrate?

____

____

____

Encouragement: If your credit report is very poor, it is only a matter of time before it gets better. If your credit report is excellent, take pride in it and keep it that way - you never know when you may need it.

Which companies do you need to contact? What improvements can you make on your credit file?

____

____

____

Chapter Seven

Where are you?

I knew I had to start somewhere, and I had to start small. The first place was my mindset. Believe it or not, that's where all the problems were. The problem wasn't that I didn't have money coming in, it was that my mind controlled what I did with it, and if the only thing I have control of is my mind then I have to start with my mind. My mind had to be right before I could change anything else.

So much is embedded within our minds and sometimes the story we fed our minds a long time ago and have forgotten about, is still influencing us. Sometimes I question myself; why save money? Why not just enjoy today? I will be okay, I'm sure it'll be alright, whenever I need money it will be alright, I'll always be alright. But how will it be alright if you don't plan for it to be alright?

My why for writing this book was the hope of helping someone else avoid the same mistakes that I made. I hope that my journey may encourage someone else to start fixing their finances. But those why's were not strong enough. The urge to write and complete this book came only when my why became closer to my heart. I want my children to have a better financial understanding and to be financially independent adults. I don't want my children to fall into the same cycle that I did. I don't want them to know about housing benefit. I want then to aim higher and to have endless possibilities. I want my grandmother to be proud of me. I want her to see my book, the book that I wrote, the amazing woman that I have become. These why's gave me momentum. These why's made me want to get out of bed and achieve my goals. They made me want to be better and do better. They gave me the comfort and strength to continue my 9 to 5 life and still put in an extra 5 hours working on my book or a business venture I was thinking about.

List your why's below:

Before I could take action, I had to first work out where I was financially. I have broken down the stages of my financial journey below.

Drowning

There was a time when I was drowning, sinking in my financial hardship to rise no more. I could not see a way out, although I knew I had to get out, I knew I was destined for better, but I waited for it as though it was going to happen by magic.

There were more payment demands than money coming in. I could not see a way out. Do I get another job? Do I borrow money so that I will then owe it to someone else? Do I give up? Do I admit defeat? I could not see a way out. When I woke in the morning, the first thing on my mind was, do I have any money in my account? How much money do I have in my account? Has a direct debit come out of my account? It was an understatement to say that I was going through a hard time, I knew I had to find a way out, and I knew I had to change my relationship with money.

My friend and I called this my drowning stage because there was no control. I had no direction or plan to keep track of how my money was spent or kept.

Floating

I got to the point that I did not want to ring the companies I owed money to because I knew I didn't have the money that I would have to promise them. At this stage of my life, I was trying to work out which debts I should be paying attention to. Which debts were keeping me up at night? I knew I should call those companies and work out a payment plan. Eventually, I was able to breathe a little because I set up those payment plans. This stage is comfortable, but it can become too comfortable, not allowing you to move on to the next stage. If you are currently at this stage with your finances, push forward to move on to the next stage. I knew I had to get to the floating stage, where I would be just about floating above the situation, above my finances, no longer drowning in debt and bills.

Even when dodging the bullets, I had to keep moving forward. I was receiving calls from bailiffs, my landlord was sending me messages, and I was receiving letters every day about a bill I hadn't paid. My sole goal was to overcome this stage and get to a place where I could have more financial flexibility.

Swimming

The swimming stage is when you feel a little freedom to move around financially - having a little money left over at the end of the month. A stage where you can take part in social activities without worrying that you are stealing from the rent money.

I took an extra job at this stage and was bringing in a little bit more income. However, I did not want to become accustomed to trading every given hour for money. At this stage, I started exploring different sources of income that might benefit me. Finding different sources of income is not as easy as it may sound, so my advice is to try to find a possibility in the things you enjoy, or the things you can do with little to no effort. I am always looking for solutions and always encouraging others to do better and be better. I do it with no effort, and the reward, when I see someone achieve a goal or a vision is priceless. I enjoyed helping people in this way and chose to take a course in life coaching and began to get paid as a life coach. I could do this and continue with my day job, therefore creating an additional income.

My other hobby is travelling. I love getting away every so often. I believe it is so important to get away from normality so that number 1 you get a break and number 2 you get to look at your life from outside the box.

My children are always my top priority. I was desperate to find ways to make money without having to leave the house or look for childcare. I enjoy searching for hotels and planning for future trips. My first online business was born out of this. www.Nextbreak.co.uk is a free comparison site for hotels, flights, taxis, and car rentals and its creation allowed me to generate passive income and therefore increase my income streams.

In the swimming stage, it is natural to try out different strokes. There is no rule that says stop dreaming whether drowning, floating, or swimming; you must continue to dream and dream big. Allow yourself to feel the fear of the possibility of your dreams coming true.

My dreams scare me; they make me wonder what if? What if I achieve the visions and goals, I have set for myself?!

Reflection: It does not matter what stage you are at, what matters is your choice to make progress.

After reading Chapter Seven what are your reflections?

Celebrations: I celebrate the fact that I can see progress and I can track my progress.
What do you celebrate?

Encouragement: only you know what stage you are at. Embrace it and aim for better.

Which stage will you be working towards?

Chapter Eight

Check List

I was tired of asking people for money.
I was tired of not having money when I needed it.
I was tired of my lifestyle, which kept me a prisoner of money.

I found that most of the money I spent went on food. Raising and feeding children is no joke financially, and food is a necessity. I did not particularly enjoy food shopping. It almost felt like daylight robbery, spending so much and then looking around a few days later and feeling that I must have dreamt I had gone food shopping. Going into the supermarket is such an experience. I would leave my house with a limited shopping list and walk out of the supermarket with bags and bags of shopping and more often than not, items from my list wouldn't even have made it into the bags. So, before I was able to manage my money better, I was that person that would hold up the queue at the checkout as I asked for items to be put back and taken off the bill. I used to have a made-up line which was 'I didn't realise I had left my other card at home'. The first time I used it was a little embarrassing, but after a while, you get over it! This is the poverty mindset and lack of financial education in action and an inefficient way of thinking. If I walked into the shop with £20 why didn't I calculate the price of items as I picked them up so that I could keep within my limit? It took a number of years, but I finally got there. However, I don't totally blame myself. It's my opinion that supermarkets have particular strategies for marketing their goods and playing with our minds. The most popular items I shopped for were bread, milk, washing up liquid and other everyday essentials. Why are these things at the back of the store in aisle 24 out of 25? Why do I have to walk past all the things I would like but can't afford before I get to the items I came to buy and most importantly, the items I need. So, I walk in with my little list, and off I go, oh, I actually wanted some yoghurt (not on my list) oh, they have a buy one, get one free offer on pizza (not on the list). A friend once told me that a bargain is something you don't need at a price you can't resist, and this is never more true than in a supermarket. I decided to test online shopping, and to my surprise, it was the answer to my problems. I was able to create a list of things I wanted, and I did not have to walk around the entire store and be enticed by items I didn't need (out of sight, out of mind). I could prepare my list days in advance and have it all delivered to my home. For me, this worked perfectly. I was able to do one big shop for essentials and most of the staple foods that keep us going throughout the month. 'Spending on food and housing make up 42% of total expenditure for households at the bottom decile of the income distribution, compared with 26% for those in the richest 10%' (ONS.GOV).[14] Food is

---

[14] Family spending in the UK - Office for National Statistics (ons.gov.uk) (https://www.ons.gov.uk/peoplepopulationandcommunity/personalandhouseholdfinances/expenditure/bulletins/familyspendingintheuk/april2018tomarch2019)

one of the biggest expenses for families and the sooner you can master a way to make savings in this area the better it is for your journey to a financial goal of just a little extra money each month.

One of my aims is to cook every other day and make enough so that the food lasts at least two days. I know some people don't like eating food cooked the day before but each to their own. As a working, studying, always on the move mum, time is in abundance as we all get 24hrs a day, and have to use it wisely. When I cook a meal on Sunday, I cook it with the intention that it will last two days. With this plan, I cook on Sunday, Tuesday, and Thursday and Saturday night is for a takeaway, or pizza in the oven, or burger and chips cooked from frozen. Having a meal plan is a vital way to save money and time. Have you ever been at work and your manager is talking to you, and you start thinking 'What am I making for dinner?' then you realise you did not take the main ingredient out of the freezer? Ha ha, this is my working mum's brain. Present but absent at the best of times. When my children were younger, I used a week A and week B timetable to mix things up, but now it is very spontaneous, especially because my 15-year-old enjoys cooking and cooks often.

I have never been faithful to one supermarket as they all have their own benefits. One of the negatives about online shopping is that some of the cheaper supermarkets don't offer this service. You have to be particular in finding the best deals for you.

At the time of writing this section of the book, it is 2020, and we are in the midst of a pandemic: the COVID-19 outbreak.

The effects of the pandemic have proven how important it is to look after your finances and save for that rainy day.

All over the news is data showing how many people have died from the outbreak and how many companies are closing down, leading to thousands of job losses. it has been a very difficult time for many people who have not been able to meet their loved ones, and for many others who have lost their jobs. Poverty is increasing rapidly. The Financial Times reported that the Department for Work and Pensions reported more than 1.8 million people had made new claims for benefits through the universal credit system since the start of March 2020.

There is no better time than now to start taking finances seriously and to learn from what we are going through. Businesses have been forced to close their doors, and many people's incomes have ceased overnight. According to the Independent Food Aid Network (IFAN) who are the UK network for independent food aid providers, '83 independent food banks distributed a total of 168,560 emergency food parcels between February and November 2019 while for February to November 2020 this figure rose to 354,613 emergency food parcels -a rise of 110%'.[15] At the same time, so many businesses have been born out of this adversity, including my free comparison site and the registration of my life coaching business. Bigger companies such as Amazon and other online business have benefited significantly since people have little option but to order online.

---

[15] Independent Food Aid Network UK (https://www.foodaidnetwork.org.uk/)

Ultimately, my financial journey has been an awesome rollercoaster ride, with tears (some of joy), happiness, freedom ... no, not the freedom, I've not reached freedom yet, but I'm on the journey. The ultimate aim is to be free from the worry caused by money, free from the worry of continuous expense, free from the worry of tomorrow and what money can buy tomorrow.

The journey to financial freedom which I continue to travel, requires new daily habits that allow you to achieve your ultimate goal.

One of the benefits of this age of technology is that there are now apps which enable you to save money. My opinion is that these apps provide a good way to save small amounts of money; sometimes the amount you save is barely noticeable, but it's put safely away from your bank account so that you are not tempted to spend it and allows you to build on small savings and continue to larger sums, as you want. I would say shop around for a trusted online saving app that will help you reach your ultimate goal.

During my research for this book, I asked a few people who have managed to secure savings or are naturally good at saving, how they do it and what skills or methods they use. The results are summarised below:

Shoebox saving - store a shoebox at the top of your cupboard or under your bed and slip in small amounts, a £10 or £5 note here and there, without keeping a record. Obviously, it should be in a secure place so that nobody else can find it.

I find this method helpful for small items such as Christmas or birthday gifts. Using this method means avoiding having to access your bank account every time you need money.

Set up a standing order from your current account to a savings account. 'The number one rule of financial understanding is pay yourself first', is a quote from John Colson's book, *The Richest Man in Babylon*. Colson advises that you pay yourself 10% of your wages before you do anything else. I'm such an advocate for this because it is you who wakes up every morning, you that had to work at your job, work for your business and work for your clients, you are responsible for doing all the work so why would you not pay yourself first? The taxman doesn't even give you a choice, so do it or make it one of your goals to be able to pay yourself first. If you cannot manage 10% start with 1% of your wages, then 2%, then 3% and so on. Begin with an amount that is comfortable and that allows you to continue to pay your priority bills.

Find a savings partner, someone you can trust and who will hold you accountable. You do not have to save large amounts; the ability to save even £100 can be the difference between asking someone else to lend you £40. You will be able to take it out of the money you have put aside with the aim of putting it back. I find it easier to keep money in bank accounts I don't have access to, or that I need to go into the bank to withdraw from. Out of sight is out of mind.

Another strategy that I find helpful is spreading my money across different accounts. I know it looks better when it is all in one place but spreading it out allows me to stop focusing so much on the amount I have saved, but to enjoy the knowledge that there is something somewhere in case it's needed.

One of my favourite tricks is working out exactly how much you need to save and how you can do it. Let's say you want to save £1,000; start by deciding how long you want to save for it and then do the calculation: for example, 1,000÷12 months tells you how much you need to save each month to achieve that goal. I like this tool because you can use it for any amount at any time to work out how much you need to put away.

Smart methods of setting goals allow you to set realistic goals that you can keep up and succeed with.

Specific	Measurable	Attainable	Relevant	Time bond
Choose a specific amount	How much do you have now? How much will you have once you reach your goal?	Set a time scale that will make your goal possible	What is your overall aim for the saved money?	When do you want to achieve this by?
£1000	£0 - £1000	12 Months x £84 a month	Towards investing in a business	Achieve by 5th April 2022

The whole point of this journey is to secure a better financial position, and it is key to think in terms of your plans. Q. What are your plans? A. I plan to get to a position of financial freedom. Start by understanding money and building a better relationship with it, and then you will be able to move to the next stage where you can start investing money to create more money that you get to keep.

I want to live the rest of my life without having to be constantly employed or dependent on others, to be able to get to a place where I am receiving a passive income and making good investments.

In the meantime, reality must be experienced and lived through. I have to take one step at a time and know that as long as I keep on improving, I will surely get there. The most important step is the first, so take the first step to begin addressing your current position. My favourite question is 'If I am blessed to live to 80 will my methods of earning and spending sustain me? Have I made provision for this?' This is my first step to understanding where I am on this journey. When I move on from this life, what am I planning to leave behind for my children? Do I have life insurance? Some people have the slight advantage of being born into wealthy families or families where money is never an issue because the generations that came before left inheritances. This is my plan, to be able to create generational wealth—to plan in a way that benefits not just the now but future generations too.

If you had all the money that you needed what kind of life would you have? Would you still be doing the job you're doing now? For me, the answer is no. Hence, I've started my journey, hence I celebrate my journey, hence I shared my journey because I have big plans. If you had all the money that you needed would you still be living in the same place?

Would you still live in the same neighbourhood? These are interesting questions to ask ourselves because self-limiting beliefs sometimes stop us from achieving what we could otherwise achieve.

I remember when I was looking for a job and couldn't find one, and for years I had convinced myself 'I can't go back to school, I can't go back to education, I don't like it, I can't write essays, oh my gosh, I struggled so much in high school with my essays, I'm not going back to education!' Yet all it took was a change of mindset. I went back to university, and I achieved a degree and a Master's. What limiting beliefs have you got that need to go?

Note down some of your limiting beliefs.

____

____

Reflection: I was convinced that I was not good at writing essays. I am no expert at them, but I was able to do what I needed to do.

After reading Chapter Eight what are your reflections?

Celebrations: I celebrate the fact that self-limiting beliefs can be removed
What do you celebrate?

Encouragement: Pay close attention to the things you want to do and the things you have talked yourself out of; there may be some form of self-limiting belief that is holding you back.

What will you be talking yourself into?

Chapter Nine

Over and Over Again

'You may encounter many defeats, but you must not be defeated. In fact, it may be necessary to encounter the defeats, so you can know who you are, what you can rise from, how you can still come out of it', American poet memoirist, and civil rights activist, Maya Angelou.

This journey took me right back to basics: 1+1 is 2, 2+2 is 4, 1-1 is 0, 1-2 equals -1 and 1-3 equals stupid. My understanding of money as numbers allowed me to set achievable goals.

While on this journey, I have failed many times, and although my situation is better now and has improved considerably, there are still moments when I slip-up and moments of learning, it would not have been a journey if I had not begun it.

At one point in my journey, I was stuck in a routine of taking out payday loans. Each month after paying it back, I would promise myself it was the last time and that I would not go back again, but, with a full heart, I went back time and time again. Eventually, this cycle became a thing of the past. I no longer need to use payday loans as I use my budget to help me work out what my monthly outgoings are each month. One of the good things about a budget is that it allows you to be flexible. When you have unexpected expenses, you can manoeuvre them to work for you. And if some months are looking short, you can look into the money you have put away for cover and not end up paying interest on a payday loan.

I can honestly say that keeping on top of my finances has been one of the most difficult things I have tried to achieve. I have completed a BA Honours degree and a Master's, but I have not been able to master financial stability as easily.

If you want to alter where your journey is taking you and achieve more, you have to be ready to step out of your comfort zone. I lived payday to payday as this was once comfortable for me.

The beauty of such a situation is that there is an opportunity for change, but the change has to begin with the mind before it can be actioned in real life.

You may find that you manage to save a little and then you have to use it for something else, but that's okay. The main point is to remember that you can do it, you can create a better financial situation for yourself and your family, you can create a better tomorrow for yourself financially and you can achieve a better relationship with money.

Reflection: It's the first steps that mean the most. Choosing to take control of a major issue in your life is very empowering'.

After reading Chapter Nine what are your reflections?

Celebrations: I celebrate never giving up, even when it seemed as though progress was not happening for me. What do you celebrate?

Encouragement: Don't give up. Just because something takes 10 years, it should not put you off. Those 10 years will come and go, and you will either have achieved your goal or be in the same situation.

What steps are you encouraged to take?

Chapter Ten

£0 to £100

How much do I top up on my electricity now? I don't. As I started working on and understanding my budget, I chose to go back to a credit metre so that I pay for electricity monthly, quarterly, or yearly. A credit metre measures how much energy you use, and your energy company bases your bill on that information.

I wanted to hold on to the key meter. I felt like the key meter meant one less bill each month. However, it was costly as the property I live in has only an electricity supply, no gas. I don't think there is anything wrong with having a pre-paid meter. The important element is to know what works for you and budget for it.

At the beginning of this book, I highlighted a statement that read '22% of UK adults have less than £100 in savings'. I am no longer part of that 22%. One hundred pounds may seem like a small amount; but don't underestimate the power of financial literacy. Becoming 'broke' could happen to anyone. As we face the COVID-19 pandemic, I don't think anyone could have predicted that 2020 was going to be such a year. There are people who are experiencing being broke for the first time, and others who are enjoying having the largest amount of money they have ever had. What I have learned whilst on my journey is that being broke is a mindset. There are many variations of poverty and not all can be defined as mindset-based; however, in relation to being broke, it is the poverty mindset that keeps you there. Throughout writing this book, I felt like it would have been much easier if I was now a millionaire. I constantly wondered why I didn't wait until I was in a better financial situation before writing this book, and I answered myself that it is not the outcome that is the exciting part, but the journey. How amazing would it be to reach out to someone who is struggling to keep £10 and help them build £100? 'Give a man a fish, and you feed him for a day. Teach him how to fish and you feed him for a lifetime', Chinese philosopher, Lao Tzu. The hope is that if we can build £100, we can build £1000 and then £10,000. And this can be achieved through forming new habits and gaining a better mindset towards money.

If you needed to borrow £10 or £20, how empowered would you feel if you could borrow it from yourself? From knowing you have something put aside for when you need it?

Take regular holidays

Holidays are such an important part of my life. A holiday doesn't necessarily mean leaving the country; it might just mean taking a break from your normal routine and seeing somewhere new. Where do I go with my £100 you ask? Save up a separate pot for your holiday or put down a deposit and pay the rest over time as you can afford it. It does not have to be an expensive holiday. It could be a hotel break in a different city in the country you live in. Allow yourself and your family to make it a priority to enjoy the small things in life. The keyword here is 'allow'. Work within your affordability, which means not splashing out on extravagant holidays just to take pictures to post on social media if your budget does not allow for it.

Create passive income

Am I lazy? I can be if I want. Do I love working? Yes, I love working with purpose, and over time I have realised that just because somebody is working hard physically or putting in more hours, does not necessarily mean they are making more money. For me, passive income means working smarter but not harder. Passive income allows you to make money whilst you sleep. It means you are not constantly trading your time for money and therefore removes the limit to how much you can make per day. I am still on my journey, and I have found two forms of passive income that are working for me. Some examples of passive income include, but are not limited to, creating a course, running a blog and affiliated marketing. I always say the Internet is everyone's best friend. You can ask it most things and you will get the answer you are looking for. Search 'passive income ideas', and the resulting lists are endless. Cash flow in family life is like the blood flow in our bodies. It is needed.

Children are expensive

Children are such a blessing, and as a parent, guardian, or responsible adult, you are financially responsible for them. In 2019 the Child Poverty Action Group (CPAG) ran a report to find the average total cost of having children.[16] They found that up to the age of 18, the cost of raising a child in a single-parent family is a staggering £185,000 compared to £151,000 for couples. Whether a single-family or couple, it is important to allow sufficient provision for this. From babies to 18-year-olds, children require many things that cost money; food, clothes, activities, childcare, education, the list goes on. I was a young adult when I had my children, and I did not give a thought to childcare fees, let alone pocket money and topping up the school lunch account years down the line. If I had known about these costs or put a plan in place, if I had had the financial literacy, maybe I would have better prepared myself. I understand the struggle of ensuring that the children's lunch accounts are topped up because it has been a struggle for me. Money affords opportunity: if you can see your child has particular skills or talents money allows you to pay to nurture these skills and talents to grow and improve. The piano lessons, the tennis lessons, the football or swimming lessons, the chef school, the dance classes, go-karting lessons etc. usually come at a cost.

The journey is about finding ways to become better and do better. As a working parent my children are not entitled to free school meals, but just because a parent is working it doesn't necessarily mean that there much disposable income. Nevertheless, let's make sure our children are focused on learning in school and not whether they can have lunch or not. Invest in your children where you can. I didn't learn to swim as a child, and I will never forget being on a ferry to the Isle of Wight and being terrified of going

---

[16] https://cpag.org.uk/policy-and-campaigns/cost-child

near the edge in case I fell into the water. For this reason, I wanted to make sure that my children learnt to swim at an early age. It was not easy or affordable, but it was a priority. As a parent, I feel that I have an opportunity now to change the level of financial education my children are exposed to. Although there are many different sources of information that could influence their future decisions, I strongly believe that charity begins at home and so do many learned habits. If I can teach them what I didn't know, that would be the way forward for the future generations of the family. I initially gave my children weekly pocket money in small amounts, £5 to £10. I have now changed to monthly payments but asked them to manage it themselves. They have sometimes failed but that is all part of the journey and hopefully a lesson that they can learn early on to avoid problems in later life.

Speak positively to and for your children, use kind words. There is power in words and some words live longer than expected. Children can be a little challenging sometimes, so try to have the patience to help them learn and grow and understand that making mistakes is a part of life and that nobody is perfect.

Look after your mental health

The state of your mental health can change very quickly, and you can sometimes find yourself in a place where you don't quite know how to manoeuvre around. Take a deep breath, stand on your two feet, and face the situation. Look at the situation as it is and work out what is the right thing to do. Sometimes the right thing is not always the easy thing. Some things happen in life that are out of our control, and some things happen as a result of our actions. For me, the glory goes to God for he has been there for me and without my faith and belief I am not sure how I would have made it this far.

I remember a time at work when I was on phone duty, and I was receiving many calls, but that morning I had received the notice for eviction, I felt so overwhelmed, and I just put my head down on my arm on the desk and started crying. No one at work knew why I was crying, and as I lifted my head, my manager saw my face covered in tears and he said, 'I know the phones can get a little overwhelming'. I just smiled and put my head back down. I said a quick prayer and had a quick word with myself, 'Agnes, you can cry at home', and continued working. Look after your mental health, look after your heart, and your mind as from these places flow the means to deal with the important issues in our lives.

The ultimate goal is to find yourself at a place where you can pay your bills and be able to do the things you want to do financially without having constant worry. To be able to sit at a dinner table with your children and your family (or by yourself) and just enjoy the moment, to be present in every moment rather than being distracted by overthinking your financial affairs. For me, it's the opening up of the mind to think of other things, not just money.

I love the array of choices we have in life; some have more choices than others, but we all have choices. To write this book was a choice. We are faced with so many choices each day; the journey is about forming the habit of making the right choices.

For some people, it could be breaking the chain of poverty, having the opportunity to change the outlook for you and your future generations. We can step into a new way of living, and this is my main aim, to help to facilitate the conversation of change. We don't have to live in lack or shortage but instead, live in abundance. We don't have to be millionaires to live in abundance. Still, we can have a different mindset which allows abundance to flow through our lives, abundance in all aspects of our lives, and this is what we need to work towards, an abundant life, abundance in your finances, abundance in your health, abundance in your well-being, abundance in your understanding, abundance in your speaking, abundance in your listening, abundance in your creativity, in your faith, abundance in your ability and abundance in the belief that you can.

Being motivated and motivating others brings great joy to my heart. I have organised and hosted two successful motivational events called 'Celebrate your Journey to Success', which brings together individuals from different walks of life and uses their stories and journeys to motivate and inspire others to follow their dreams. I also make a weekly encouragement voice post on Tuesdays called 'choose day', just a short 2-minute message aimed at voicing encouragement.

One question I ask you today is 'What is stopping you from becoming the best version of yourself? What is stopping you from achieving your goals, your visions your dreams? What is stopping you from following through with what it is you believe deep inside you are called to do?'

When I decided to write the final part of the book, I gave myself ten weeks and I took myself out of my everyday life. I told my friends and family that I would not be available for ten weeks because I had to give birth to my book. One thing that has helped me get to where I am now is understanding that you have to surround yourself with the right people, people that are on the same mission as you are and people that are going to help you accelerate to your next level. Unfortunately, that is sometimes easier said than done.

At the time of writing my book there was no one in my immediate circle, who I could seek advice from; therefore, there was no one I could call on. I had to separate myself from my circle and take time out to research YouTube, read other books for motivation, and use the Internet to get the information that I needed to complete my book.

Action will always give results, but you have to put in the work to get those results. I had to put the words into this book to have a complete book. I had to research this subject and record my journey to get the results, which is the end product, 1+1 = 2, action equals results. The results may be positive or negative, depending on the action itself.

I told some people that the book would be ready for pre-order in 10 weeks, so save £1 per week and you will be able to purchase a copy. This same formula can be used to achieve so many things and especially, to reach the £100 mark. You just have to be able to break it down backwards. How much divided by how long = the small steps needed to achieve the goal.

I have had the opportunity to see how people who have good credit and savings walk and talk. Financial literacy comes with a form of confidence. The confidence to know that you can cover all your bills, you can walk into a showroom and purchase a car on credit if you want to because you have an excellent credit rating; the confidence to know you can provide for your children's needs financially; the confidence to know you can support your children if they wish to go to university or require a large deposit for an expensive purchase: you are in a position to gift them this. I have not yet achieved this level of freedom but forgetting what is behind me and reaching forward to those things which are ahead, I press forward every day with faith and believe that it will happen for me and for you.

If it is going to be done, you're going to have to do it. If there is some object or outcome you want in your life, it's up to you to activate it, to achieve what it is you want to achieve. It's not going to be easy, but it's possible: choose to believe in yourself; choose to believe in your vision; choose to believe in your goals; choose to believe you can and choose to believe it can happen for you.

If you can believe it, then you can achieve it: choose to invest in yourself; choose to invest in your idea; invest time to invest knowledge; invest in a network of people that can help you and remember it is never too late as long as you are still breathing; it is never too late to reach for the stars; to start working on your dream; to start working on your goals today; to start speaking of your vision today; choose to start; it is better that you start and find a way to finish, than 'never starting' because you cannot work out how.

At my last graduation, none of the friends or family I invited were able to make it, so it was myself and my two sons. As I walked across the stage to receive my certificate, I realised that this was the moment I had worked towards for the previous two years and that, more than anyone, it was my children who had witnessed the stress and hard work that entailed. As I looked up, I knew that I had to ensure the two of them should reap the benefits of all my hard work. To change my relationship with money was a choice I had to make to break a cycle that could be passed on through generations.

Being broke is not something that most people are exempt from. You can have the highest paying job, but if you don't have the financial education to help you understand how to keep your money (because it's not about how much you make but how much you keep) you can find yourself in a place where you are struggling financially. There are many different reasons why people find themselves in financial hardship. The hope is that we can have more open and honest conversations about money so that there's a clear vision of hope for all.

I have recently invested in some stocks, although not a huge amount. I have read about stock investments, and I understand it's a gambling game. For my own education and understanding, I invested in a few different companies and got the kids involved in suggesting them.

One of the best feelings is getting a notification that I have made money, whether it is via eBay (the buying and selling app) or Depop (a peer-to-peer social shopping app) to say I have made a sale or earned a commission on a booking through NextBreak.co.uk, or a sale of my personal development course. It is especially good to wake up to such notifications knowing I made money whilst I was sleeping. It is not the amount that matters so much, especially when you are starting off, but the consistency in finding and working on different forms of passive income. I have big dreams, and I hope to eventually move on to bigger investments, such as property. It is all a journey and having confidence in how far I have come, I have faith that this too will happen.

The secret to living is to give, to share some of what you have - it does not have to be much. Whether you are giving to your church, to your family or to a charity - give. Choose to find a way to give something back, even if it just your time. Giving comes with many blessings.

Reflection: I am grateful for my journey.

After reading Chapter Ten what are your reflections?

____

____

____

____

____

____

Celebrations: the hope of helping you on your journey
What do you celebrate?

____

____

____

Encouragement: Start small, start today, start now!

What steps will you be taking from here?

____

____

____

____

Challenge

Congratulations on reaching the end of the book and for saving some money!

Remember, the amount is not the most important element, although the more money you have at the end the better opportunities you can engage in.

£1 × 10 = £10

£5 × 10 = £50

£10 × 10 = £100

Out of the money you have put aside, I challenge you to use 10% as a starting point for a savings fund.

Take another 10% and find a way to bless someone with it, gift it to the church or to a charity.

Now choose a percentage of the money left over and see how you can make that amount grow. If you have £10 in total, you have put aside £1 for savings, you have blessed someone with £1 and you have £8 to work with. This is where the internet becomes useful. With £8 you could buy several small items and resell them online for a profit. You could buy fractional shares in a company, or you could make a few containers of food to sell for profit to family and friends. It is about using your imagination to make each coin birth a new coin. You may not feel comfortable doing any of these things; however, success is mostly found outside of our comfort zone.

You also have the option to hold on to the money you have saved and continue to do the same thing, put money aside often and grow your savings. Getting better is the main aim.

Remember this is for you and your own journey. Consistency is key. Never give up on what you really want.

Closing notes

'Addicted to being Broke' is a focus on mindset and lack of financial education and how they affect an individual stuck in a cycle of never-ending debt or living in lack. Struggling to provide for yourself or your family is not part of the plan of any hard-working person or anyone who aims to be a provider for their family. So, when you are faced with an endless lack of money or are in a position where you are constantly running out of money it can become very frustrating and demotivating. The cycle of earning just to spend can easily become a habit that has no benefit. The quicker you are able to identify such a pattern in your life the quicker you can start working your way out of it.

I am hoping this book removes the stigma of being broke and gives us a platform to discuss our finances and help each other. There was a time when going to the gym was not the talk at the table, where being overweight was looked at in a different light, but now, thanks to the talks at the table and a better understanding of how food impacts bodies differently, we are able to talk about food, gym, workouts, health benefits and so much more on the subject. My hope is that one day, starting as young as possible, children will be taught the importance of understanding money and how that understanding will benefit them, especially in the future when they are adults in charge of making and managing their own money and providing for the next generation.

I am still on my journey and someone who is more financially literate than I, may pick up on some of the things I have written and think that I still have a poverty mindset. I encourage you to share your knowledge and enlighten others.

Call to action: what the reader should do after completing this book.

I encourage you to start keeping track of your spending, have respect for your hard-earned cash and constantly ask yourself what else you could be doing with your money. Talk about your struggles with somebody who can help you. Share your knowledge if you can help someone else. Sometimes we make the issue bigger in our own minds, but its only when we share our experience with others, we get a real view of how small our problems may be.

Printed in Great Britain
by Amazon

60784510R00061